Change

A Choral Dialectic
for Unaccompanied SATB Choir

- Secretary Michael

"Change"
Choral Dialectic
by Secretary Michael

ISBN: 978-1-888712-37-7

What is a Choral Dialectic?

A "choral dialectic" is a four-movement choral work (with or without instruments) in which a rational argument about any subject is battled-out musically. There's only one rule: every choral dialectic must use the following four titles for its four movements:

1. "PRINCIPLE"
Each dialectic begins with a statement of some sort. This will be the subject matter for the entire work. Oftentimes the statement is an ideal - an expression of how something might be in a perfect world.

2. "ARGUMENT"
In this movement, the "Principle" begins its journey through the meat grinder. The Argument's job is to pick apart the principle, either supporting it or challenging it.

3. "COUNTERARGUMENT"
In this movement, the "Principle" gets supported or challenged again, but this time from a contrasting perspective. If the previous argument was sweet, this one will probably be sour. If the previous was about abundance, this one will probably be about scarcity.

4. "RESOLUTION"
Now that the "Principle" has been analyzed from different angles, some sort of final understanding will have to emerge. Maybe there will be growth, a new way of being, a new way of living in the world, a new "Principle". Or maybe not.

Machinists Union Press
web: www.machinistsunion.org
email: twimfina@gmail.com

Change

Duration: Less than 12 minutes

Principle

(from the "Change" choral dialectic)

Words and Music: Secretary Michael
Opening hymn is from the Secular Hymnal (Hymn #111)
Reharmonized by Secretary Michael

♩=80

D Gmaj7 Em7 F#m B7 Em7 A A7 D

S: Things are the way they are,_____ and not the way they're not._____ Things

A: Things are the way they are_____ and not the way they're not._____ Things

T: Things are the way they are_____ and not the way they're not._____ Things

B: Things are the way they are_____ and not the way they're not._____ Things

5

D Gmaj7 Em7 F#m B7 Em7 A A7 D

S: go the way they go,_____ and stop the way they stop._____ Un -

A: go the way they go,_____ and stop the way they stop._____ Un -

T: go the way they go,_____ and stop the way they stop._____ Un -

B: go the way they go,_____ and stop the way they stop._____ Un -

9

A   D   A   F#7   Bm   C#7   F#m   F#m7

S: til we make the change, it should not be for - got: Things

A: til we make the change, it should not be for - got: Things

T: til we make the change, it should not be for - got: Things

B: til we make the change, it should not be for got: Things

W17 ("We believe" passage, measure 17)

♩=96

13

B   G+ B7 Em7   G Gmaj7 Em7   A7(sus4) A7   D   D

S: are the way they are, and not the way they're not.

A: are the way they are, and not the way they're not.

T: are the way they are, and not the way they're not. We be-lieve that change is good when

B: are the way they are, and not the way they're not. We be-lieve that change is good when

18

A   A[7]   D   A   A[7]

S

A

T: it brings peace and bro-ther-hood. Let this be our ob-li-ga-tion. Let this be our de-sti-na-tion.

B: it brings peace and bro-ther-hood. Let this be our ob-li-ga-tion. Let this be our de-sti-na-tion.

C21 *("Change" passage, measure 21)*

21

D   Em

S: When life be-comes un-fair.

A: When life be-comes un-fair.

T: Change, change, change, change, change. Change, change, change, change,

B: Change, change, change, change, change. Change, change, change, change,

Measure 24:

S: For peo - ple a - ny - where. When there is suf - fer - ing,__

A: For peo - ple a - ny - where. When there is suf - fer - ing,__

T: change. Change, change, change, change, change.

B: change. Change, change, change, change, change.

C29

Measure 27:

S: these are chan ges we can bring, and that's the rea-son why we sing. Change, change, change, change,

A: these are chan ges we can bring, and that's the rea-son why we sing. Change, change, change, change,

T: Change, change, change, change, Change, change, change, change. Choo-choo-choo-choo-choo-choo-choo-choo-

B: Change, change, change, change, Change, change, change, change. Choo-choo-choo-choo-choo-choo-choo-choo-

30
Em
S
change.
Change, change, change, change, change.
A
change.
Change, change, change, change, change.
T
Our train is mo - vin' fast. Choo-choo-choo-choo-choo-choo-choo-choo We're mo - vin' from the past.
B
Our train is mo - vin' fast. Choo-choo-choo-choo-choo-choo-choo-choo We're mo - vin' from the past.
33
A
D
S
Change, change, change, change, change. Let this be our ob - li - ga - tion.
A
Change, change, change, change, change. Let this be our ob - li - ga - tion.
T
Choo-choo-choo-choo-choo-choo-choo-choo Come join us at the sta- tion! Let this be our ob - li - ga - tion.
B
Choo-choo-choo-choo-choo-choo-choo-choo Come join us at the sta- tion! Let this be our ob - li - ga - tion.

W37

36

S *Let this be our de-sti-na-tion. We be-lieve that change is good when it brings peace and bro-ther-hood.*

A *Let this be our de-sti-na-tion. Change, change, change, change, Change, change, change, change,*
(clap) (clap) (clap) (clap)

T *Let this be our de-sti-na-tion. We be-lieve that change is good when it brings peace and bro-ther-hood.*

B *Let this be our de-sti-na-tion. We be-lieve that change is good when it brings peace and bro-ther-hood.*

C41

39

S *Let this be our ob-li-ga-tion. Let this be our de-sti-na-tion. Change, change, change, change,*
(clap) (clap)

A *Change, change, change, change, Change, change, change, change. Change, change, change, change,*
(clap) (clap) (clap) (clap) (clap) (clap)

T *Let this be our ob-li-ga-tion. Let this be our de-sti-na-tion. Choo-choo-choo-choo-choo-choo-choo-choo.*

B *Let this be our ob-li-ga-tion. Let this be our de-sti-na-tion. Choo-choo-choo-choo-choo-choo-choo-choo.*

10

W49

Let this be our de-sti-na-tion. We be - lieve that CHANGE! good when it brings peace and CHANGE! hood.
(clap) (clap) (clap) (clap) (clap) (clap)

Let this be our de-sti-na-tion. We be CHANGE! change is good when it brings CHANGE! bro-ther - hood.
(clap) (clap) (clap) (clap) (clap) (clap)

Let this be our de-sti-na-tion. CHANGE! lieve that change is good when CHANGE! peace and bro-ther - hood.
(stomp) (stomp) (stomp) (stomp) (stomp) (stomp)

Let this be our de-sti-na-tion. We be - lieve that change is CHANGE! it brings peace and bro-ther CHANGE!
(stomp) (stomp) (stomp) (stomp) (stomp) (stomp)

H53 ("Horn" passage, measure 53)

Let this be our CHANGE! ga-tion. Let this be our CHANGE! na-tion. Oo Oo
(clap) (clap) (clap) (clap)

Let this CHANGE! ob-li - ga-tion. Let this CHANGE! de-sti - na-tion. Grab your hat and tie your shoes, our
(clap) (clap) (clap) (clap)

CHANGE! be our ob-li - ga-tion CHANGE! be our de-sti - na-tion. Oo Oo
(stomp) (stomp) (stomp) (stomp)

Let this be our ob-li CHANGE! Let this be our de-sti CHANGE! Oo
(stomp) (stomp) (stomp) (stomp)

H57

Soprano: Oo / Choo! Choo! Choo! / Oo / Oo / Oo / We! Must! Do!

Alto: train is chug-ging Choo! Choo! Choo! Chug-ging off with me and you to make the chang es We! Must! Do!

Tenor: Oo / Choo! Choo! Choo! / Oo / Oo / Oo / We! Must! Do!

Bass: Oo / Choo! Choo! Choo! / Oo / Oo / We! Must! Do!

Soprano: Oh / Oh / Oh / Song! We! Know! / Oh / Oh

Alto: Chug-ging fast or chug-ging slow, this chug-ging is a Song! We! Know! Sing it high and sing it low, now

Tenor: Oh / Oh / Oh / Song! We! Know! / Oh / Oh

Bass: Oh / Oh / Song! We! Know! / Oh

(train horn) (train horn) (train horn) (train horn)
60 Am E° E° E° A7
S
Oh Here! We! Go! Song! We! Know! We! Must! Do! Choo! Choo! Choo! Choo! Choo! Choo! Choo! Choo!
A
all to-ge-ther Here! We! Go! Song! We! Know! We! Must! Do! Choo! Choo! Choo! Choo! Choo! Choo! Choo! Choo!
T
Oh Here! We! Go! Song! We! Know! We! Must! Do! Choo! Choo! Choo! Choo! Choo! Choo! Choo! Choo!
B
Oh Here! We! Go! Song! We! Know! We! Must! Do! Choo! Choo! Choo! Choo! Choo! Choo! Choo! Choo!
W63
63 D A A7 D
S
We be-lieve that change is good when it brings peace and bro-ther-hood. Let this be our ob-li-ga-tion.
A
We be-lieve that change is good when it brings peace and bro-ther-hood. Let this be our ob-li-ga-tion.
T
We be-lieve that change is good when it brings peace and bro-ther-hood. Let this be our ob-li-ga-tion.
B
We be-lieve that change is good when it brings peace and bro-ther-hood. Let this be our ob-li-ga-tion.

W67

66

S — Let this be our de-sti-na-tion. We be-lieve that change is good when it brings peace and bro-ther-hood.

A — Let this be our de-sti-na-tion. Change, change, *(clap)* change, *(clap)* change, Change, change, *(clap)* change, *(clap)* change,

T — Let this be our de-sti-na-tion. We be-lieve that change is good when it brings peace and bro-ther-hood.

B — Let this be our de-sti-na-tion. We be-lieve that change is good when it brings peace and bro-ther-hood.

C71

69

S — Let this be our ob-li-ga-tion. Let this be our de-sti-na-tion. Change, change, *(clap)* change, change, *(clap)*

A — Change, change, *(clap)* change, change, *(clap)* Change, change, *(clap)* change, change. *(clap)* Change, change, *(clap)* change, change, *(clap)*

T — Let this be our ob-li-ga-tion. Let this be our de-sti-na-tion. Choo-choo-choo-choo-choo-choo-choo-choo.

B — Let this be our ob-li-ga-tion. Let this be our de-sti-na-tion. Choo-choo-choo-choo-choo-choo-choo-choo.

72

Em

S: change. Change, change, *(clap)* change, change, *(clap)* change.

A: change. Change, change, *(clap)* change, change, *(clap)* change.

T: *(stomp)* Our train is mo-vin' fast. Choo-choo-choo-choo-choo-choo-choo-choo. We're mo-vin' from the past. *(stomp)*

B: *(stomp)* Our choo-choo train is fast. Choo-choo-choo-choo-choo-choo-choo-choo. We're mo-vin' from the past. *(stomp)*

75

A⁷   D

S: Change, change, *(clap)* change, change, *(clap)* change. Let this be our ob-li-ga-tion. *(clap)* *(clap)*

A: Change, change, *(clap)* change, change, *(clap)* change. Let this be our ob-li-ga-tion. *(clap)* *(clap)*

T: Choo-choo-choo-choo-choo-choo-choo-choo. Come join us at the sta-tion! *(stomp)* Let this be our ob-li-ga-tion. *(stomp)* *(stomp)*

B: Choo-choo-choo-choo-choo-choo-choo-choo. Come join us at the sta-tion! *(stomp)* Let this be our ob-li-ga-tion. *(stomp)* *(stomp)*

W79

78

S: Let this be our de-sti-na-tion. We be - lieve that CHANGE! good when it brings peace and CHANGE! hood.
(clap) *(clap)* *(clap)* *(clap)* *(clap)* *(clap)*

A: Let this be our de-sti-na-tion. We be CHANGE! change is good when it brings CHANGE! bro-ther - hood.
(clap) *(clap)* *(clap)* *(clap)* *(clap)* *(clap)*

T: Let this be our de-sti-na-tion. CHANGE! lieve that change is good when CHANGE! peace and bro-ther - hood.
(stomp) *(stomp)* *(stomp)* *(stomp)* *(stomp)* *(stomp)*

B: Let this be our de-sti-na-tion. We be - lieve that change is CHANGE! it brings peace and bro-ther CHANGE!
(stomp) *(stomp)* *(stomp)* *(stomp)* *(stomp)* *(stomp)*

81

S: Let this be our CHANGE! ga - tion. Let this be our CHANGE! na - tion.
(clap) *(clap)* *(clap)* *(clap)*

A: Let this CHANGE! ob - li - ga - tion. Let this CHANGE! de - sti - na - tion.
(clap) *(clap)* *(clap)* *(clap)*

T: CHANGE! be our ob - li - ga - tion. CHANGE! be our de - sti - na - tion.
(stomp) *(stomp)* *(stomp)* *(stomp)*

B: Let this be our ob - li CHANGE! Let this be our de - sti CHANGE!
(stomp) *(stomp)* *(stomp)* *(stomp)*

83
D
S
A
T
B
(Clap&Stomp)
We be - lieve that change is good!
(Clap&Stomp)
We be - lieve that change is good!
(Clap&Stomp)
We be - lieve that change is good!
(Clap&Stomp)
We be - lieve that change is good!

Argument

(from the "Change" choral dialectic)

Words and Music: Secretary Michael

("Oo" passages sung lighter than the text passages)

Measures 9–12:

S: Oo / Oo / Oo / Oo

A: Oo / Oo / Peo-ple they got sick and were cough ing e-v'ry-where. / Peo-ple who seem dif-f'rent got left out in the cold.

T: Oo / Oo / Oo / Oo

B: Dirt was in our food__ and dirt was in our air. Oo / Oo
peo-ple who got in-jured and peo-ple who grew old.

Measures 13–16:

S: Look at all the things that change has done. It has gi-ven hope to e - v'ry - one.

A: Look at all the things that change has done. It has gi-ven hope to e - v'ry - one.

T: Look at all the things that change has done. It has gi-ven hope to e - v'ry - one.

B: Look at all the things that change has done. It has gi-ven hope to e - v'ry - one. Like

17
C Am G C C Am G C
S
Me too! Choo- choo!
A
Like me. Like me.
T
And me. We're the train!
B
me. Like me. Like-a
21
C Am G C Am G C C Am G C
S
Choo choo! Choo choo! Choo choo!
A
Chug ga choo! Chug ga choo! Chug ga choo!
T
Like a me. Chug ga me. Chug ga chug ga
B
me. Chug ga me Chug ga chug Chug ga
24
C Am G C
S
Choo - choo!
A
Chug - ga choo choo choo choo choo
T
Chug - ga chug chug chug chug
B
chug - ga chug - ga chug - ga chug - ga chug - ga chug - ga chug - ga chug - ga

Measure 25:

S: Choo – choo!

A: choo Chug – ga choo choo choo choo choo

T: chug chug chug Chug – ga chug chug chug chug

B: chug – ga chug – ga chug – ga chug – ga chug – ga chug – ga chug – ga chug – ga

Measure 26:

S: Choo – choo!

A: choo Chug – ga choo choo choo choo choo

T: chug chug chug Chug – ga chug chug chug chug

B: chug – ga chug – ga chug – ga chug – ga chug – ga chug – ga chug – ga chug – ga

Measure 27:

S: Choo – choo! Choo! Choo! Choo! Choo!

A: choo Chug-ga choo choo choo choo choo Choo! Choo! Choo! Choo!

T: chug chug chug Chug-ga chug chug chug chug Choo! Choo! Choo! Choo!

B: chug-ga chug-ga chug-ga chug-ga chug-ga chug-ga chug-ga chug-ga Choo! Choo! Choo! Choo! chug-ga

29 | C | Am | G | C | C°7

S: Choo - choo! Choo! Choo! Choo! Choo!

A: choo Chug-ga choo choo choo choo choo Choo! Choo! Choo! Choo!

T: chug chug chug Chug-ga chug chug chug chug Choo! Choo! Choo! Choo!

B: chug-ga chug-ga chug-ga chug-ga chug-ga chug-ga chug-ga chug-ga Choo! Choo! Choo! Choo!

31 | C°7 | C | G#°7 | Am | C°7 | C | Dm | G7 | C

S: Look at all the things that "change" has done. It has gi-ven hope to e - v'ry - one.

A: Look at all the things that "change" has done. It has gi-ven hope to e - v'ry - one.

T: Look at all the things that "change" has done. It has gi-ven hope to e - v'ry - one.

B: Look at all the things that "change" has done. It has gi-ven hope to e - v'ry - one.

Performance Note: To make the story clear, the 5 singers in this movement should be standing away from the main choir to help convey that they are a different group with a very different point of view.

Counterargument

(from the "Change" choral dialectic)

Secretary Michael

10
G A7 Bm Em A7 D
T solo
al - ways be pro - tec - ted be cause e - v'ry time I make this pro - mise, I get re - e - lec - ted.
T 2 men
dum - my, dum my dum dum - dum dum - dum dum - dum dum. So the
B 2 men
dum - my, dum my dum dum - dumm... dum - dumm... dum - dumm... dum. So the
13
G D A7 Bm G A7 Bm Em
T solo
T 2 men
back - ward things we al - ways do will al - ways be pro - tec - ted be - cause e - v'ry time he makes this pro - mise,
B 2 men
back - ward things we al - ways do will al - ways be pro - tec - ted be - cause e - v'ry time he makes this pro - mise,
16
A7 D
T solo
T 2 men
he gets re - e - lec - ted. No more change! No more change! No more change!
B 2 men
he gets re - e - lec - ted. No more change! No more change! No more change!

(spoken slowly, with a sarcastic whiny voice feigning sorrow)
20
D
Bm7
T solo
Mayor (solo): The peo - ple want - ing change, their train broke down!
T 2 men
No more change! dum - my dum dum
B 2 men
No more change! dum dum
(spoken slowly, with a sarcastic whiny voice feigning sorrow)
23
(resume tempo)
G6
A
A7
(laughter.......) And their choo - choo - choo - choo - choo - choo does - n't e - ven make a sound!
(laughter.......) dum - my dum dum
(laughter.......) dum dum
26
(resume tempo)
G D A7 Bm G A7
(laughter.......) They should learn the les - son that they should have learned when they were small: that they
(laughter.......) dum - my, dum - my, dum - my, dum - my, dum - my, dum - my dum
(laughter.......) dumy - my, dum - my, dum - my, dum - my, dum - my, dum - my dum

29

Bm   Em   A⁷   D   G D A⁷ Bm

T solo: can - not fight a gainst our rights and can't fight Ci - ty Hall.

T 2 men: dum-dum dum-dum dum-dum dum. They should learn the les-son that they should have

B 2 men: dum- dumm... dum- dumm... dum- dumm... dum. They should learn the les-son that they should have

32

G   A⁷   Bm   Em   A⁷   D

T 2 men: learned when they were small: that they can - not fight a-gainst our rights and can't fight Ci - ty Hall.

B 2 men: learned when they were small: that they can - not fight a-gainst our rights and can't fight Ci - ty Hall.

35

T solo: *Mayor (solo):* If

T 2 men: No more change! No more change! No more change! No more change!

B 2 men: No more change! No more change! No more change! No more change!

Measure 39:

T solo: some-one has a pro-blem, they should come and take a look, 'cuz we al-ways have the an-swer in our

T 2 men: dum-my dum dum   dum-my dum dum   dum-my dum dum

B 2 men: dum   dum   dum   dum   dum   dum

Measure 42:

T solo: Ci-ty Hall Book. In our Ci-ty Hall Book, life is per-fect-ly ar-ranged, so we

T 2 men: dum-my dum dum   dum-my dum dum   dum-my dum dum

B 2 men: dum   dum   dum   dum   dum   dum

Measure 45:

T solo: ne-ver, ne-ver, ne-ver, ne-ver, ne-ver have to change.

T 2 men: dum-dum   dum-dum   dum-dum-dum. In our Ci-ty Hall Book, life is

B 2 men: dum-dum   dum-dum   dum-dum   dum. In our Ci-ty Hall Book, life is

48
Em A7 Bm Em A7 D
T solo
In our
T 2 men
per - fect - ly ar - ranged, so we ne - ver, ne - ver, ne - ver, ne - ver, ne - ver have to change. In our
B 2 men
per - fect - ly ar - ranged, so we ne - ver, ne - ver, ne - ver, ne - ver, ne - ver have to change. In our
51
G F♯m Em A7
T solo
Ci - ty Hall Book, life is per - fect - ly ar - ranged,
T 2 men
Ci - ty Hall Book, life is per - fect - ly ar - ranged, so we
B 2 men
Ci - ty Hall Book, life is per - fect - ly ar - ranged,
54
D A7 D
T solo
ne - ver, ne - ver, ne - ver, ne - ver, ne - ver have to change.
T 2 men
ne - ver, ne - ver, ne - ver, ne - ver, ne - ver have to change.
B 2 men
ne - ver, ne - ver, ne - ver, ne - ver, ne - ver have to change.

Resolution

(from the "Change" choral dialectic)

Words and Music: Secretary Michael

Lyrics:

S / A: We who work for Change, we have a rule_ of thumb:

T / B: The change we want to change must be the

S / A: If we can not change our-selves, we can't change a - ny - one._

T / B: change that we be - come." The

7 — Em7 / A / A7 / D

T: change we want to change must be the change that we be - come." We

B: change we want to change must be the change that we be - come." We

Assertively (Alto)
Assertively (Bass)

A (line 2): We

9 — F# / Bm / F# / Bm

S: Oo_____ Oo_____

A: wrote these books, we can write 'em a - gain. They were writ-ten by wo-men, they were writ-ten by men. When the

T: wrote these books, we can write 'em a - gain. They were writ-ten by wo-men, they were writ-ten by men. When the

B: wrote these books, we can write 'em a - gain. They were writ-ten by wo-men, they were writ-ten by me._ When the

11 — E / A / E / A

S: Oo_____ Oo_____

A: laws of the land lead to pain and de - spair, we have a du - ty to change 'em and to make them fair!

T: laws of the land lead to pain and de - spair, we have a du - ty to change 'em and to make them fair!

B: laws of the land lead to pain and de - spair, we have a du - ty to change 'em and to make them fair!

Measure 13:

But be fore we shout for change, be - fore we bang our drum. (S)

But be fore we shout for change, be - fore we bang our drum. (A)

The change we want to change must be the (T)

The change we want to change must be the (B)

Measure 16:

We're the most im-por-tant change, the change we must get done. (S)

We're the most im-por-tant change, the change we must get done. (A)

change that we be - come. The (T)

change that we be - come." The (B)

Measure 19:

Assertively

We (A)

change we want to change must be the change that we be - come." We (T)

Assertively

change we want to change must be the change that we be - come." We (B)

21

S: Oo_____ Oo_____

A: wrote these books, we can write 'em a-gain. They were writ-ten by wo-men, they were writ-ten by men. When the

T: wrote these books, we can write 'em a-gain. They were writ-ten by wo-men, they were writ-ten by men. When the

B: wrote these books, we can write 'em a-gain. They were writ-ten by wo-men, they were writ-ten by me._ When the

23

Alto Solo: Things

S: Oo_____ Oo_____

A: laws of the land lead to pain and de-spair, we have a du-ty to change 'em and to make them fair!

T: laws of the land lead to pain and de-spair, we have a du-ty to change 'em and to make them fair!

B: laws of the land lead to pain and de-spair, we have a du-ty to change 'em and to make them fair!

(Soloist must be clearly audible over the main choir)

Alto Solo (m. 25): are | the | way | they | are,_____ | and | not | the | way | they're

S (m. 25): We who work for Change, we have a | rule__ of thumb:

A (m. 25): We who work for Change, we have a | rule__ of thumb:

T (m. 25): The change we want to change must be the

B (m. 25): The change we want to change must be the

Alto Solo (m. 28): not._____ | Things | go | the | way | they | go,_____ | and

S (m. 28): If we can not change our-selves, we can't change a-ny-one.__

A (m. 28): If we can not change our-selves, we can't change a-ny-one.__

T (m. 28): change that we be - come." | The

B (m. 28): change that we be - come." | The

34

♩=96
41
D
A
A7
D
S
We be lieve that change is good when it brings peace and bro-ther- hood. Let this be our ob - li - ga tion.
A
We be lieve that change is good when it brings peace and bro-ther- hood. Let this be our ob - li - ga tion.
T
We be lieve that change is good when it brings peace and bro-ther- hood. Let this be our ob - li - ga tion.
B
We be lieve that change is good when it brings peace and bro-ther- hood. Let this be our ob - li - ga tion.

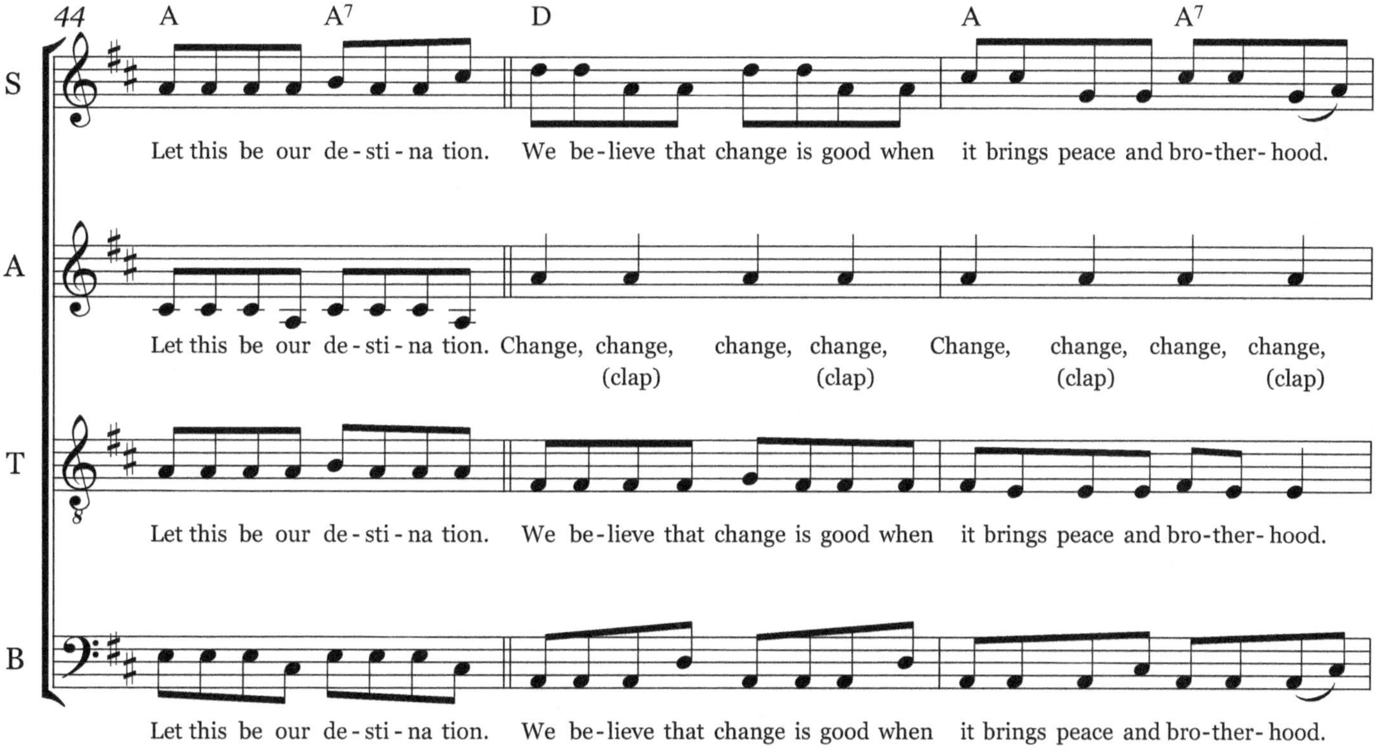
44
A
A7
D
A
A7
S
Let this be our de - sti - na tion. We be - lieve that change is good when it brings peace and bro-ther- hood.
A
Let this be our de - sti - na tion. Change, change, change, change, Change, change, change, change,
(clap) (clap) (clap) (clap)
T
Let this be our de - sti - na tion. We be - lieve that change is good when it brings peace and bro-ther- hood.
B
Let this be our de - sti - na tion. We be - lieve that change is good when it brings peace and bro-ther- hood.

47

D

S: Let this be our ob-li-ga tion. Let this be our de-sti-na tion. Change, change, change, change, (clap) (clap)

A: Change, change, change, change, Change, change, change, change. Change, change, change, change, (clap) (clap) (clap) (clap) (clap) (clap)

T: Let this be our ob-li-ga tion. Let this be our de-sti-na tion. Choo-choo-choo-choo-choo-choo-choo-choo.

B: Let this be our ob-li-ga tion. Let this be our de-sti-na tion. Choo-choo-choo-choo-choo-choo-choo-choo.

50

Em

S: change. Change, change, change, change, change. (clap) (clap)

A: change. Change, change, change, change, change. (clap) (clap)

T: Our train is mo-vin' fast. Choo-choo-choo-choo-choo-choo-choo-choo. We're mo-vin' from the past. *(stomp)* *(stomp)*

B: Our choo-choo train is fast. Choo-choo-choo-choo-choo-choo-choo-choo. We're mo-vin' from the past. *(stomp)* *(stomp)*

S (m. 53): Change, change, change, change, change. (clap) (clap) Let this be our ob-li-ga-tion. (clap) (clap)

A (m. 53): Change, change, change, change, change. (clap) (clap) Let this be our ob-li-ga-tion. (clap) (clap)

T (m. 53): Choo-choo-choo-choo-choo-choo-choo-choo. Come join us at the sta-tion! *(stomp)* Let this be our ob-li-ga-tion. (stomp) (stomp)

B (m. 53): Choo-choo-choo-choo-choo-choo-choo-choo. Come join us at the sta-tion! *(stomp)* Let this be our ob-li-ga-tion. (stomp) (stomp)

S (m. 56): Let this be our de-sti-na-tion. (clap) (clap) We be-lieve that CHANGE! good when (clap) (clap)

A (m. 56): Let this be our de-sti-na-tion. (clap) (clap) We be CHANGE! change is good when (clap) (clap)

T (m. 56): Let this be our de-sti-na-tion. (stomp) (stomp) CHANGE! lieve that change is good when (stomp) (stomp)

B (m. 56): Let this be our de-sti-na-tion. (stomp) (stomp) We be-lieve that change is CHANGE! (stomp) (stomp)

58

A   A⁷   D

S: it brings peace and CHANGE! hood. Let this be our CHANGE! ga - tion.
(clap)   (clap)   (clap)   (clap)

A: it brings CHANGE! bro - ther - hood. Let this CHANGE! ob - li - ga - tion.
(clap)   (clap)   (clap)   (clap)

T: CHANGE! peace and bro - ther - hood. CHANGE! be our ob - li - ga - tion.
(stomp)   (stomp)   (stomp)   (stomp)

B: it brings peace and bro - ther CHANGE! Let this be our ob - li CHANGE!
(stomp)   (stomp)   (stomp)   (stomp)

60

A   A⁷   D   (Clap&Stomp)

S: Let this be our CHANGE! na - tion. We be-lieve that change is good!_____
(clap)   (clap)

A: Let this CHANGE! de-sti - na-tion. We be-lieve that change is good!_____
(clap)   (clap)   (Clap&Stomp)

T: CHANGE! be our de-sti - na-tion. We be-lieve that change is good!_____
(stomp)   (stomp)   (Clap&Stomp)

B: Let this be our de-sti CHANGE! We be-lieve that change is good!_____
(stomp)   (stomp)   (Clap&Stomp)

Recent Works by Secretary Michael

Jo Puma - Wild Choir Music

Collection of 36 traditional "Sacred Harp" arrangements with new secular lyrics for our diverse society. This collection has removed the 3 barriers that have kept this music out of our schools: inappropriate lyrics, poor shape-note legibility, and nonstandard use of standard solfege names. Now we all have a chance to experience this exciting early American music. (Book available; check for free download: www.machinistsunion.org/works.html)

Secular Hymnal

Collection of 144 favorite hymn tunes from around the world. The hymn tunes have been re-notated and given thoughtful egalitarian lyrics that promote peace. Many public schools use them for choral sight-reading practice. Available in both unison/guitar and SATB choir editions. Now we all have a chance to share in these musical treasures. (Books available; check for free download: www.machinistsunion.org/works.html)

Twimfina

A peace-themed musical play for singing groups of all ages. The story is about a young woman named "Twimfina" (an acronym for "The World Is My Family, I'm Not Afraid") who runs off to a hostile country. It is scored for voice and piano. The play is divided into 21 segments, many of which can stand alone. This allows an acting group to perform individual segments instead of the entire 2.5 hour play. (Book available; check for free download: www.machinistsunion.org/works.html)

Choral Dialectics

A "choral dialectic" is a 4-movement choral work (with or without instruments) in which a rational argument is battled-out musically. There's only one rule: every choral dialectic must use the following four titles for its four movements: "Principle" - "Argument" - "Counterargument" - "Resolution"
Secretary Michael has begun working on a series of 6 choral dialectics, some of which are available now; the rest will become available as they are completed in future years. (Books available; check for free downloads: www.machinistsunion.org/works.html)

Aren't We the Lucky Ones

A book-length story about a group of college science students who share an understanding that people don't truly have a free will. There are no "good people" or "bad people", just lucky and unlucky ones. This insight carries with it the responsibility to protect the "unlucky" from the wrath of the "lucky". The students form a community in order to live out their ideals. (Book available - both paperback and digital).

Joy of Piggyback Songs

Dozens of fun, short choral works in which more than one melody is sung at the same time. Book (and free internet download) will become available after it is completed.

"Please help create public choirs that are free from religious and nationalistic content so that all singers feel welcome."

- Secretary Michael

www.ingramcontent.com/pod-product-compliance
Lightning Source LLC
Chambersburg PA
CBHW080535030426
42337CB00023B/4738